Getting Closer

Getting Closer

WILLIAM L. COLEMAN

BETHANY HOUSE PUBLISHERS
MINNEAPOLIS, MINNESOTA 55438
A Division of Bethany Fellowship, Inc.

Published by Bethany House Publishers
A Division of Bethany Fellowship, Inc.
6820 Auto Club Road, Minneapolis, Minnesota 55438

Printed in the United States of America

Library of Congress Cataloging-in-Publication Data

Coleman, William L.
   Getting closer / William L. Coleman.
      p.   cm.
    1. Married people—Religious life. 2. Intimacy—Religious aspects—Christianity—Meditations.   I. Title.
    BV4596.M3C65   1988
    242'.64—dc 19
ISBN 1-55661-039-4 (pbk.)   88–21120
                                                    CIP

*To
Pat
after
25*

William Coleman

has been married for over twenty years. For ten years as a pastor he counseled many couples during their dating, engagement, and marriage. He has also helped couples whose marriages are in trouble and others who have gone through a divorce.

With his experience as a researcher, writer and speaker, he communicates effectively in the area of family relationships. He has authored nearly three dozen books on a variety of topics.

Contents

PEN UP

Marriage has never been a good place to hide. The more we share our deep and honest feelings, the happier our relationship will be. But it isn't easy. Opening up takes time and practice. The closer we come to revealing the real person, the smoother our love life will run. Every day we can learn a little more about our partner.

God made billions of fascinating people, and you are getting to know one of them intimately. Have a great time watching one of God's treasures open up.

Bill Coleman

Aurora, Nebraska

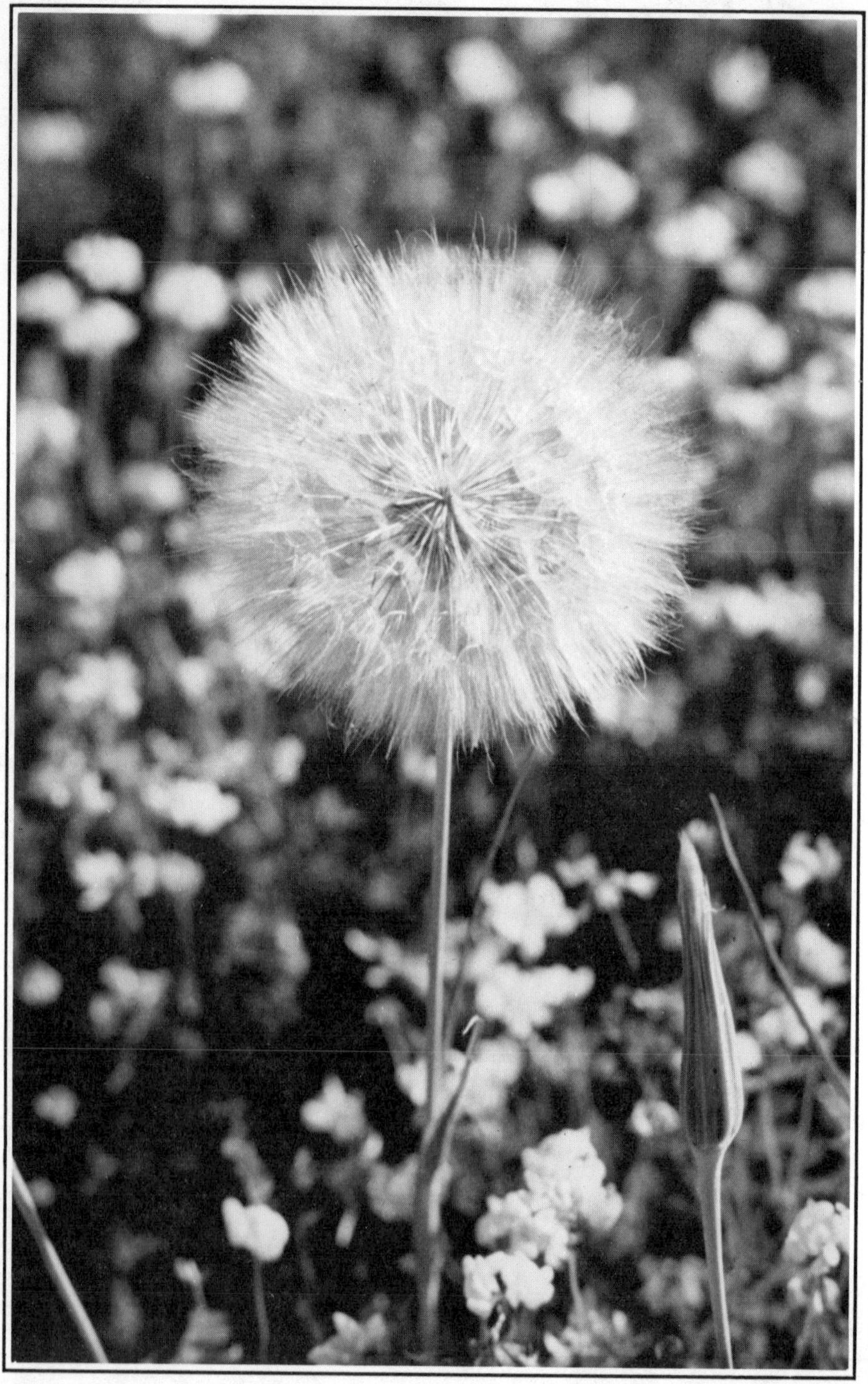

THE GENTLE COUPLE

Christ taught us
To be gentle,
To calm down,
To hold,
To touch.

Christ taught us
To be gentle,
Not to push
Or shake,
Never to hurt
Or hit.

Christ taught us
To hold our anger
To short spurts,
To manageable
Conversations.

Christ taught us
To forgive,
To understand,
To make up,
To make right.

Christ taught us
To be gentle,
Not to push
Or shake,
Never to hurt
Or hit.

"Let your gentleness be evident to all."

Philippians 4:5

PROMISE TO PRAY

I promise to pray
For you.

I will ask God
To set you free.
Free to be you,
Free to rise up
To where
You want to be.

I will ask God
To travel the road
With you,
To protect you
In mind,
In body,
In spirit.

I will not ask God
To change you
To match my
Expectations.

I did not marry you
To make you into
Someone else.

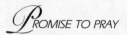

I will ask God
To minimize your fears,
To increase your joy,
To honor your dedication,
To strengthen your faith.

I will ask God
To bless your love,
To encourage your playfulness,
To multiply your service,
To enhance your kindness.

I will ask God
To set you free.
Free to be you,
Free to rise up
To where
You want to be.

"And I pray that you, being rooted
and established in love, may have
power, together with all the saints,
to grasp how wide and long and
high and deep is the love of Christ."
Ephesians 3:17, 18

DRAGGING GRASSHOPPERS

Even grasshoppers
Must have days
When they barely
Drag along.

They can't hop
Every day,
All day long.

Don't they stop
Sometimes
And lean
Against a stalk
Or lie down
On a leaf?

They can't chew
Every day,
All day long.

This grasshopper
Runs out
Of hop
Every once
In a while.

Try to understand.
Some days
This grasshopper
Is simply
Out of hop.

"And the grasshopper drags himself
along."

Ecclesiastes 12:5

SOLOMON WAS A RASCAL

Solomon may have been
A rascal
But he had the right
Idea.

He and the Mrs.
Liked to sneak away
From the palace
Once in a while
And spend a night
In the village.

The text spares us
The details
But every married couple
Can imagine
The happy little scene.

They probably checked in
At the Desert Sands Motel
For a mini-honeymoon,
The little rascals.

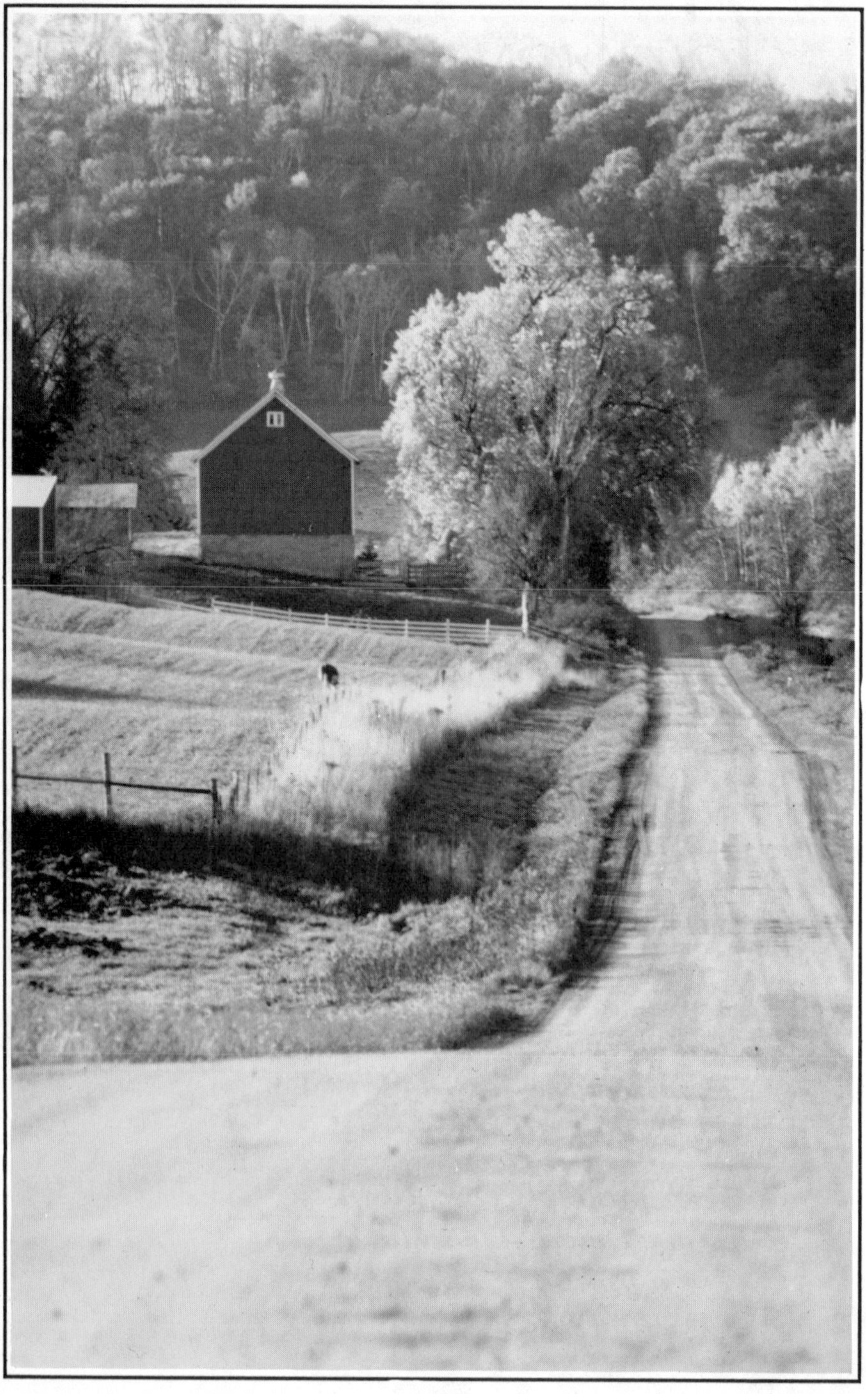

Complete with a carry-out meal—
A few goat burgers
And half a gallon
Of warm camel milk—
They locked the tent
And spent the night
In the village.

No wonder the Mrs.
Was nuts
About the King.

"Come, my lover, let us go to the
countryside, let us spend the night
in the villages."
                    Song of Solomon 7:11

CHASING THE WIND

Thanks for having enough sense.
Thanks for being real.
Thanks for refusing to chase
Pretense and prestige.

Our goal was never to "wow" everyone.
We never tried to turn people's heads
By what we owned.
Our goal was never to collect as much
As we could.

Thanks for being genuine
And refusing to
Chase the wind.

"This too is meaningless, a chasing
after the wind."

Ecclesiastes 6:9

*S*ULKING, MOPING AND POUTING

We aren't always mature.
Sometimes our communications
Fall apart.
That's when we turn to
Sulking, moping and pouting.

It isn't a pretty picture.
Like children, we retreat
To separate corners
In the house.

I slither into the basement,
And you head for the bedroom.

We sit and steam,
Imagine nasty things
We would like to say,
Scores we want to settle,
Clever little quips
We would like to deliver.

Not great role models
For the children.
Not the behavior two adults
Could brag about.

Just two lovers
Trying to cope
In our own
Awkward way.

As time goes by
We grow more,
We talk more,
We mope and pout
Less.

Sulking, moping and pouting
Waste too much time
When we could be talking,
Listening and loving.

"He lay on his bed sulking and
refused to eat."

1 Kings 21:4

LET'S GO HOME

Let's go home
And tell them
How good God
Has been.

Let's go to our
Seafront cottage,
Row house
Or condominium,
To our apartment,
Duplex, split-level,
Or RV by the road,
And let's tell them
How good God
Has been.

We will tell
Our wives
And hug them
Till they hug back.

We will tell
Our husbands
And run
Our fingers
Through their hair.

We will tell
Our children,

Tussle with them
On the floor,
Hold hands
At the table
While we pray.

We will not be silent.
That wouldn't be fair.
We will not
Leave them guessing
Why we are happy.

Let's go home
And tell them
How good God
Has been.

"Return home and tell how much
God has done for you."
Luke 8:39

*A*LWAYS TRUE

Don't believe everything
You hear
About adultery and affairs
And flings and trysts.

Not everyone dabbles
With dalliances.
Not everyone searches for
The forbidden fruit.

Don't believe everything
You see
On TV.
Don't let every survey
Make you wonder.

It's tough to be faithful
In a mobile,
Fast-moving world.
But it's possible,
And it's being done
By millions.

Don't be confused
By "Dallas";
Don't be influenced
By songs;
Don't be bewildered
By statistics.

It's tough to be faithful,
But
It works for millions
Of us.

"Let love and faithfulness never leave you; bind them around your neck, write them on the tablet of your heart."

Proverbs 3:3

SEPARATED

*Cars and wheels
Were not made
To be separated.*

*Neither runs well
Without the other.*

*Try to imagine
Birds without wings.
Picture a ladder
Without rungs.*

*They weren't meant
To be separated.*

What would
Roses be
Without petals,
Or trees
Without roots?

What are radios
Without sound?
Try to draw
Mountains
Without height.

Can you dream
Of an earth
With no sun?

They weren't meant
To be separated.

And neither are we.

"Therefore what God has joined
together, let man not separate."
Matthew 19:6

HE LID

There is one thing
She wants to say,
One intimate thought
She wants to whisper
In your ear.

But she isn't sure
How to word it,
How to phrase it
In soft, creative
Terms.

She needs to say it
Because there is danger.
She has to say it
Because it grinds her.

But she loves you
Too much
To take the risk.

And so
We will say it
For her.

Put the lid down.

"Love is kind."
1 Corinthians 13:4

29

Macho—Who Needs It?

If macho means only
He can lie on
His stomach in the mud
And hunt ducks—
Who needs it?

If macho means
He can cuss,
Throw fits,
And pick
Chicago Bear scores—
Who needs it?

If macho means
Cold, stiff,
Self-centered,
Steel-eyed,
And bossy,
She can live
Without it.

But if manly means
Gentle, patient,
Helpful, kind,
And thoughtful,
She can't get enough.

If manly means
He thinks of her,
Puts up storm windows,
Sets tables,
Holds her,
And sits through musicals,
She can't get enough.

Macho is a facade,
A lobster
With a tough shell.

Manly means
He cares,
Is gentle,
And isn't afraid
To show it.

"For I am gentle and humble in heart." Matthew 11:29

RESPECT FOR SILENCE

Watch the leaves
Fall quietly
And never say
A word.

Watch the dusk
Engulf the yard
And never make
A sound.

Watch the sun
Slide slowly away
And never breathe
A whisper.

Sometimes it's better
Not to talk.
Sometimes it's better
To gather strength
From the silence.

Don't insist,
Don't prod,
Don't demand,
Don't push.

Just sit
And feel each other's
Presence.

Words will only
Get in the way.

My burden is heavy,
My confusion is real.
My mind has trouble
Sifting out the facts.

Most of the time
It is better to talk.
But not this time.

It's better now
To simply be
Silent.

"Let him sit alone in silence, for the
Lord has laid it on him."   Lamentations 3:28

ℒONELY AIRPORTS

It's tough to be
In a lonely airport
At the end of
A rough week.

You have been
Rerouted,
Reticketed,
Rescheduled,
Reissued,
Rejected
And
Regurgitated.

Tired and dejected,
You know you won't
Make it home
Again tonight.

Feeling sorry
For yourself,
You see
A young creature
Standing alone
By the snack shop.

And she looks fine
And gentle
And soft,

And for a moment
You wonder.

And for a moment
You wonder.

But, thank God,
You remember
The brown eyes
That are waiting
For you.

You remember
That crazy grin
And a voice
That would warm
A rock.

You remember
What you promised her
Forever and forever.

And you cuddle up
On a green plastic bench
With yesterday's
Denver Post.

"Who keeps his oath even when it hurts."

Psalm 15:4

DIVORCE IS A MYTH

Parents are never divorced.
They merely stop
Living together.

Parents are tied together
By a human life.
As long as they care,
As long as they love
That child,
They will never be divorced.
They merely stop
Living together.

He thought he would
Get rid of his wife,
File papers,
Move out.

She imagined she could
Cut him from her life,
Hire a lawyer,
Make a settlement.

But
Parents are never divorced.
Loving a child
Ties them together.

"And he and his wife are united so that they are no longer two, but one. And no man may separate what God has joined together."
Mark 10:8, 9, TLB

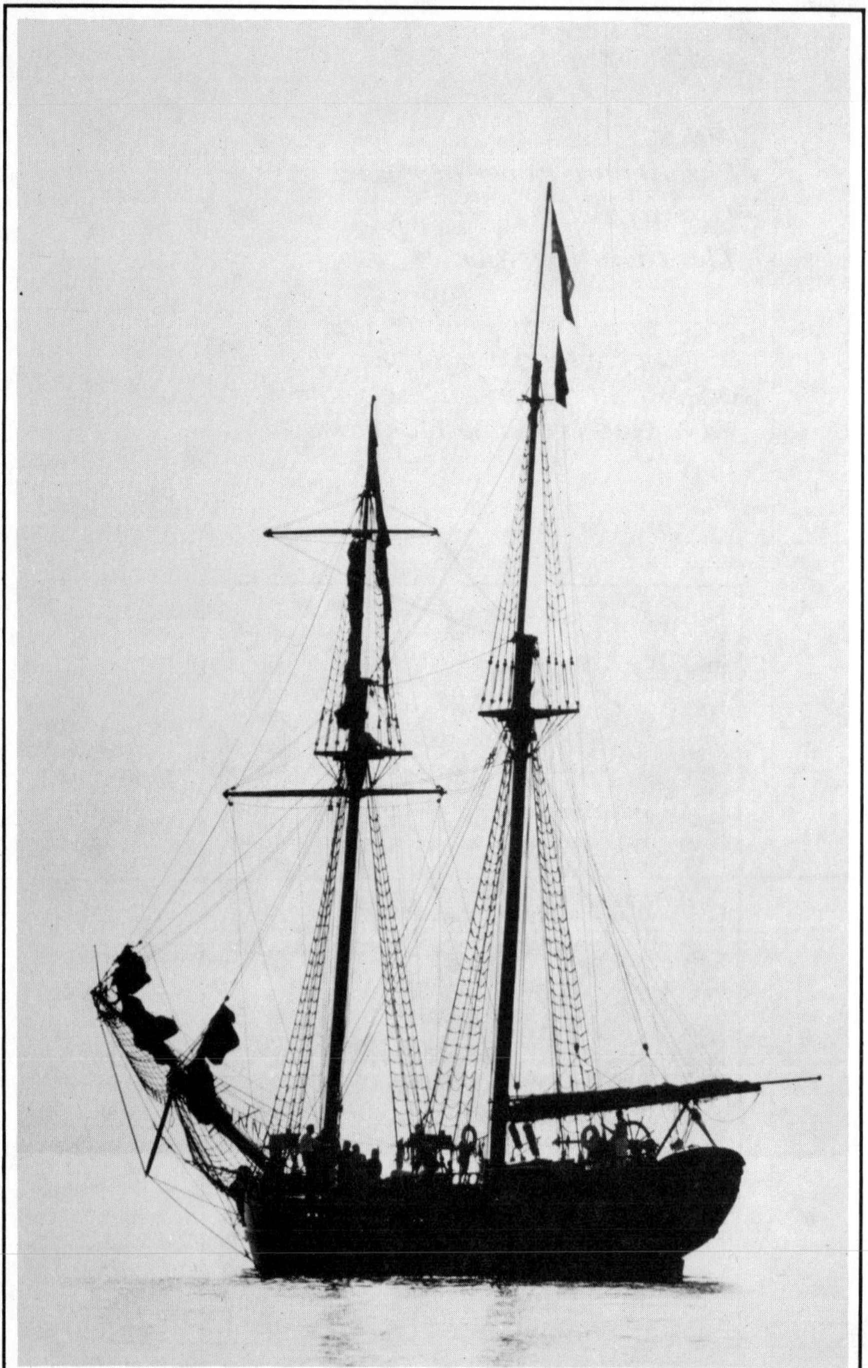

EMPTY DREAMS

Don't speak to me
Of mountains
We will never climb.
Don't make me hope
For oceans
We will never sail.

Don't tell me about
Far-off dreams
That we will never
Make come true.

We can't live on
Travel brochures,
Road maps
And blueprints.

Don't tease me
With plans
That will never
Happen.

Give me one weekend
In a canoe
Rather than five years
Of empty dreams.

I'd rather have
Two days in Omaha
That years of promises
About the Scotland
We will never see.

Don't be afraid
To decide.
Don't push
Each dream
Away.
Don't raise
My hopes
Only to let them
Shrivel again.

Don't become
My shallow angel
Who delivers
Empty dreams.

Couples cannot
Thrive
On hollow promises.

"Like clouds and wind without rain
is a man who boasts of gifts he
does not give."
                    Proverbs 25:14

$\mathcal{L}$OVE TALK

When you're in love,
You say a lot
Of silly things.

Like:
"I'll help with the dishes"
Or
"I don't like expensive
Things"
Or

"Hamburger is just fine
With me."

When you are locked
Arm-in-arm
You say,
"I don't care where
We live,"
Or
"Money doesn't mean
Anything to me"
Or
"You look good
In a sweat suit."

Even Solomon,
Old butter-tongue himself,
Said things like
"Your navel is
A rounded goblet."

That probably turned
Her heart to
Pomegranate mush.

The crazy things
People say
When they're
In love.

Song of Solomon 7:2

NEVER GAVE IT A THOUGHT

Some partners worry
About their mates.
They worry
Where they might go,
What they might say,
Whom they might see,
What they might become
Involved in.

But some of us
Never gave it a thought.

We don't sit and fret
Over what our mates
Might say behind our backs.

We don't pace the floor
Wondering where they are
And what they might
Be doing.

We love each other
And we
Never gave it a thought.

We never stayed awake
In an empty bed
Afraid to think
Of whom they might be with.

We could have stewed
And tormented
And let our imaginations
Run wild.

But we love each other
And we
Never gave it a thought.

Instead of worrying
We sleep together,
We talk together,
We work together,
We cry together.

But we don't
Worry away the night
Wondering about
Faithfulness.

We love each other
And we
Never gave it a thought.

"Love . . . always trusts."
1 Corinthians 13:7

# DISCOURAGEMENT

She asked him,
"When do we stop trying?"
And he said,
"It's too soon."

She asked him,
"When do we look
For other things to do?"
And he answered,
"We will work harder."

She asked him,
"How long do we
Hope and pray?"
And he replied,
"As long as it takes."

She asked him
If he ever became
Discouraged.
And he responded,
"Yes!
But only for
A moment."

She asked him
No more.
She joined in
And they both
Reached for
The goal.

"David also said to Solomon his son, 'Be strong and courageous, and do the work. Do not be afraid or discouraged, for the Lord God, my God, is with you.' "
1 Chronicles 28:20

ROLLING IN BED

When you get up early,
Why do I roll
To your side of the bed?
And why do you roll
To mine?

Is it because the other side
Is warm or comfortable?
But both sides are
Warm and comfortable.

Or do we roll
Because we enjoy
The very scent of
The one we love?

Barely awake,
We fill up our senses
With the one
We love every day.

Our senses tell us
Love is beautiful,
Love is secure,
Love is satisfying.

Even while we
Are apart,
We still gain
Strength
From the one
We love.

No one leaves
The scent
Our lover
And partner
Has.

God made
Our partner
Unique.

"My beloved is to me a cluster of
henna blossoms from the vineyards
of En Gedi."

Song of Solomon 1:14

∫OLID PLANNING

Step-by-step,
Let's invest
And build
Some solid
Security.

Solid Planning

A little something
For our old age,
Maybe a few dollars
For our dream house.

Let's not buy stock
In purple popcorn
Or radio-shoes,
Nor invest in
Liver soup
Or spinach-flavored
Gum.

Step-by-step,
Let's keep
Our heads.
Put away
A dollar here,
A quarter there.

No wild schemes
For square eggs,
Cement airplanes,
Or
Coffee-ground
Suckers.

Nothing quick,
Speedy,

And no
"Sure thing."

We are building;
We aren't gambling.

Step-by-step,
Let's put it
Away.
Let's create
A tad of
Security.

"He who works his land will have abundant food, but the one who chases fantasies will have his fill of poverty."

Proverbs 28:19

$\mathcal{I}$T WASN'T FUNNY

Usually I'm a pretty funny guy.
I can make faces, imitate birds
And I can remember jokes
From the 7th grade.

But what I said last night
Wasn't very funny.

Usually I'm a pretty funny guy.
I can make maps of Israel
Out of mashed potatoes
Or sing two stanzas of
"I won't go huntin' with you, Jake."

I can remember David Letterman jokes,
Bill Cosby skits, Harry Anderson tricks.
I have a game with wooden sticks
That is a total riot.

But what I said last night
Wasn't very funny.

I didn't mean to hurt you.
I didn't even know
I hurt you,
But I did.

Thanks for being understanding,
Forgiving and patient.
Maybe someday I'll get
Better material.

Because what I said last night
Wasn't very funny.

"Nor should there be obscenity,
foolish talk or coarse joking, which
are out of place, but rather
thanksgiving."
Ephesians 5:4

LOTTED OUT

Smart couples know how
To blot out things
They don't want to remember.

Burnt food, missed planes,
Remarks about our hair,
Broken cups, spilled coffee,
Jokes about our clothes.

Some couples take the time
To memorize mistakes,
To embroider them
On their minds.

Some couples know
The dates, the weather,
The company, the occasion
When the insult was made.

Smart couples blot out
The details,
Cover over the words,
Mark out the feelings.

*B*LOTTED OUT

It's a method
They learned
From God.
He is busy
Blotting out
Our mistakes,
Our crimes,
Our sins.
And God is
A good teacher.

Smart couples don't keep
A ledger of complaints
Against the ones
They love.

They blot out
Each mistake
The way God
Taught them.

"I, even I, am he who blots out your
transgressions, for my own sake,
and remembers your sins no more."
Isaiah 43:25

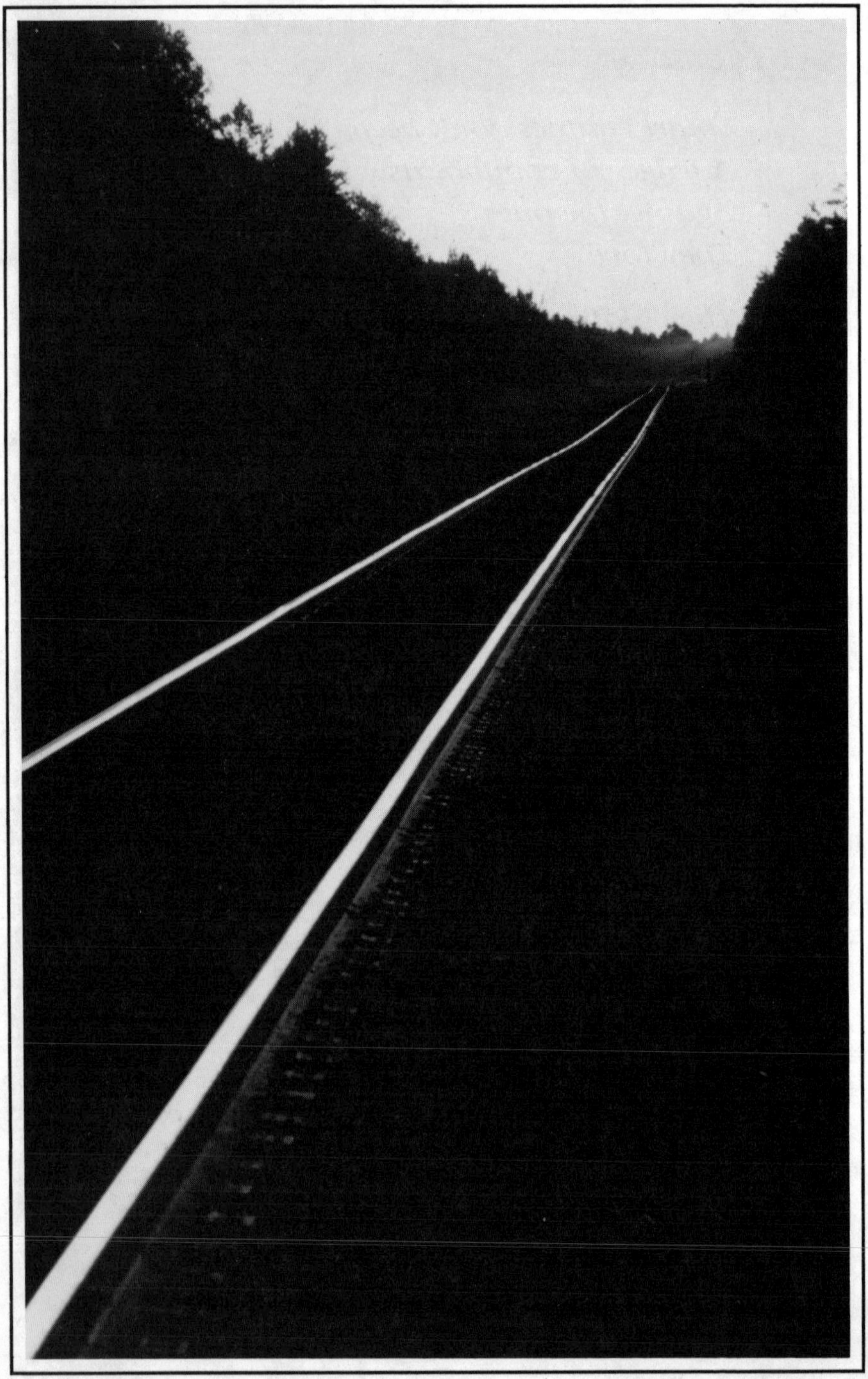

JUST COOL IT!

We are racing
Ninety miles an hour.
Our hearts are pumping,
Our feet are running.
We need to be everywhere
All at once.

There are clocks to watch,
Schedules to keep,
Projects to complete,
Meetings to attend.
We need to do everything
All at once.

We are hurrying
Past each other
In a mad race
To nowhere.

Let's slow it down
Before we wake up
And find
One of us missing.

Let's take time and
Just cool it!

God wants us
To get to know
Each other.

"A relaxed attitude lengthens a
man's life."   Proverbs 14:30, TLB

# BAGGAGE

She carried
A lot of baggage
Into her marriage.

She had
A bad experience
With an old boyfriend.

She had
A dad
Who forgot
To be loving.

During her awkward years,
She felt like a klutz
And was hard on herself.

She carried
A lot of baggage
Into her marriage.

Treat her gently
When she starts
To get strung out.

Speak softly
When she's sad
And wants to sit
Awhile.

BAGGAGE

Help her sift out
The past,
And help her forget
The things that
Trap her.

She carried
A lot of baggage
Into her marriage.

"Forget the former things; do not
dwell on the past."
Isaiah 43:18

DAVID WAS A GOOD OL' BOY

If you are a man,
You have to like David.

He killed a nine-foot
Philistine foreflusher
With a sling and sword.

David was macho.
He lived on the cutting edge,
Took adventure
Where he found it.

When a lion stole
One of his sheep,
David went after him,
Grabbed the lion
By the scruff of the neck
And killed him.

He then turned on a bear
And with a couple of swift jabs
Took the smile off
Big Ben's face.

David was a man's man.
He was tough,
He was cool,
He was solid.
David was a good ol' boy.

And David did us all
A serious favor
When he admitted
That sometimes
He was afraid.

And it was all right
To be afraid

And to admit that
He was afraid.

Sometimes David trembled
Like a loose shutter
On a windy night.

The same way we do
When our child is sick,
When we can't pay the bills,
When our job folds up,
When our tests come back
Positive.

And we stand alone
On the back porch
Tight-lipped,
Staring blankly
At the trees.

David was a tough ol' boy.
And sometimes he was afraid
And it was all right
For him to say so.

"Fear and trembling have beset me;
horror has overwhelmed me."
            Psalm 55:5

ARE YOU GROWING WITH ME, JESUS?

Some days all of us wish
We were more mature,
A tad more stable,
A little more dependable,
Just a millimeter more level.

Presidents, soldiers, actors,
Anchorwomen, department heads,
Purchasing agents, cowboys,
And basket weavers.

All of us wish
We could stand
A little firmer
Day in and day out.

Even Jesus had to grow up
And become wiser
And more mature.

I don't understand that.
Why did Jesus have to
Grow up?
But I'm glad He did.
It makes me feel better
All over.

If Jesus had to grow up,
He understands people who
Have to grow up.
Even people who are older,

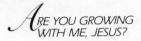
Married, parents and titled.
Even couples who are seasoned,
Experienced and established.

Every day I want
To become more mature
And gain a balance
In life.

Almost every day
It's a struggle,
And I need to know
That Jesus is helping me
Grow up.

"And Jesus grew in wisdom and
stature, and in favor with God and men." Luke 2:52

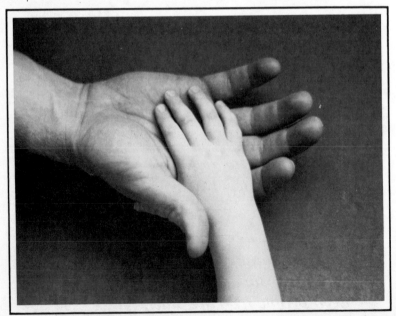

BLENDING

She loved to go for it;
He liked to think it over.
She wanted to jump in the car
And take off;
He needed maps, reservations and
A plan from Triple A.

She enjoyed a little debt;
He longed for security.
She wanted to scuba dive;
He liked reading on the beach.

She always wondered what
It was like to explore caves;
He never did.

But they loved each other
And they wanted to go
Together
At the same speed.

So he began to accelerate,
Went on donut runs
At midnight,
Rode on snowmobiles
And went tubing.

So she slowed a notch,
Tried to warn him
What was coming,
Called him two hours
Before they boarded a plane.

She moved more cautiously
And he picked up the pace.

Their schedules began to match
Inch by inch and day by day,
And they began to blend
Because they loved each other.

"Love does not demand its own
way."

1 Corinthians 13:5, TLB

TAKING VOWS

No one should
Take vows lightly.
A promise
Is a promise.

Captains do not resign
Midway through the voyage.
Pilots do not refuse
To land their planes.

Painters who remove
A canvas only half
Finished
Are not really painters.

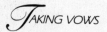

Most composers
Rework their composition
Until it takes
A sturdy form.

Vows made
To each other,
Vows made
To God,
Vows made
To ourselves
Are vows
We work hard
To keep.

No one should
Take vows lightly.
A promise
Is a promise.

"When a man makes a vow to the
Lord . . . he must not break his
word. . . ."
                        Numbers 30:2

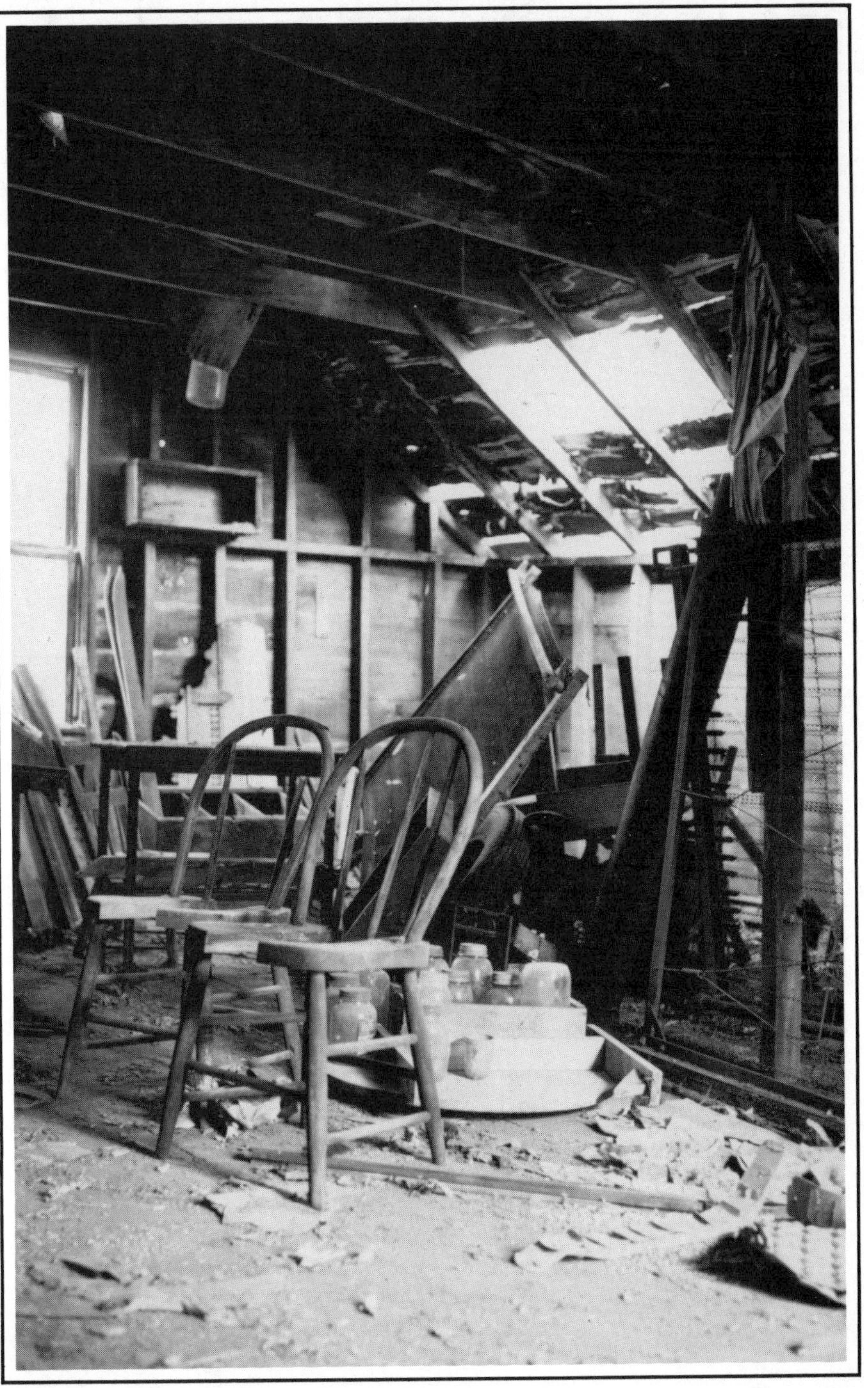

ONE-WOMAN MAN

Men think
They have to roam.
No matter what
It takes,
They imagine they

*Must find
New conquests,
New adventures,
New affairs.*

*Men believe it
Because
Men want to
Believe it.*

*No matter what
The penalties,
The guilt,
The hurt,
The disease,
The disloyalty,
The sin,
No matter what,
They think they
Have to
Branch out.*

*Men convince themselves
That their
Manhood demands it,
That their
Physical needs can't wait,
That
It's only normal.*

But they forget
The loyalty
They promised
To the one
Back home.

It may be hard
To be
A one-woman man,
But it's worth
The struggle
To be loyal to
The one he loves.

"But a man who commits adultery
lacks judgment; whoever does so
destroys himself."

Proverbs 6:32

KEEP THE RUBIES

Who can find a wife
Of noble character?

A wife who resists gossip?

Who doesn't spend her time
Clawing her way up
The social ladder?

Who doesn't push to be seen
With the right people?

Who doesn't brood over
Invitations she didn't receive?

Who can find a wife
Of noble character?

Keep the rubies.
I think I found her.

A wife who takes clothes
To the poor.

A wife who cares for
Her own business.

Who reaches out to
Prisoners, immigrants, children,
Her family, students and the elderly.

Who mends, cooks, cleans,
Hikes, snowball fights, gives,
Shovels, prays and snuggles.

Who can find a woman
Of noble character?

Keep the rubies.
I think I found her.

"A wife of noble character who can
find? She is worth far more than
rubies."

Proverbs 31:10ff.

OPPING OFF

We don't need to pop off
To prove we are tough.
We don't need to blow up
To get our way.

Couples in love learn
To control their anger
And pump up their affection.

Some little boys think
Real men have to scream,
Shout and have tantrums
When they grow up.
They never grow up.

Some little girls believe
Real women are ratty,
Demanding and obnoxious
When they become adults.
They never become adults.

Couples in love don't
Need to spend
A lot of time
Popping off.

They measure their response,
They weigh their words
And maintain the temperature.

When they need to confront,
They confront,
Balancing that confrontation
With enough love
To smother a teddy bear.

"The Lord is compassionate and
gracious, slow to anger, abounding
in love."

Psalm 103:8

DOCTOR OF WORDS

Heavenly Father,
Give me a gift
That I may become
A Doctor of Words.

Teach me to say
Words that will
Give my spouse a lift
And a reason
To hope.

Give me a phrase,
Sincere and honest,
That will help her
Believe
When it would be easier
To doubt.

Keep me from words
Of despair
That only tear a soul
Apart.

Give me the prescriptions
That bring cheer,
That create optimism,
That restore faith.

When her bones are tired
And her spirit is worn out,
Let me be the one
Who brings her renewed strength
And a fresh set of dreams.

Help me listen,
Help me hear
What really
Bothers her
Beneath the symptoms.

Show me how
To point her
Toward
The sunshine
Well beyond
The clouds.

Heavenly Father,
Give me a gift
That I may become
A Doctor of Words.

"Pleasant words are a honeycomb,
sweet to the soul and healing to the
bones."

Proverbs 16:24

THE STUBBORN ZONE

What do you think
When she stops talking
And stares out the window?

What do you think
When she looks at you
With one eye squinted
Half-closed?

You know she has stopped
Reasoning and
Entered the stubborn zone.

What do you think
When he says, "We'll see,"
Or he changes the subject?

How do you feel
When he gets up
And walks into the other room?

You know he has stopped
Reasoning and
Entered the stubborn zone.

What can you do
When your spouse drops out
Of the discussion?

Do you yell,
Pound the table,
Tear up his newspaper,
Put prune juice
In his coffee?

Do you move
To the couch
And put crackers
On her side of the bed?

Do you buy
An ad
On cable TV
Asking her to talk?

It isn't nice
To fool with
A relationship
By hiding
In our
Stubborn zone.

"For I knew how stubborn you
were; the sinews of your neck were
iron, your forehead was bronze."
Isaiah 48:4

*S*HOUTING AND CHEERING

Let's make a promise,
Take a vow,
From this moment on
Starting today.

We are going to
Build each other up
Rather than
Pull each other down.

We are going to remind
Each other
What our strengths are.
We are going to talk
About encouragement,
Progress, hope and faith.

We are going to applaud
Each other,
Cheer, shout, give awards,
Hug, kiss, brag,
Pick each other up
Off the floor
(If we can).

We are going to encourage
Each other
To go for it,
To take the risk,
To dare to be
All we possibly can.

Let's make a promise,
Take a vow,
From this moment on
Starting now.

We are going to
Build each other up
Rather than
Pull each other down.

"Building you up rather than pulling
you down."

2 Corinthians 10:8

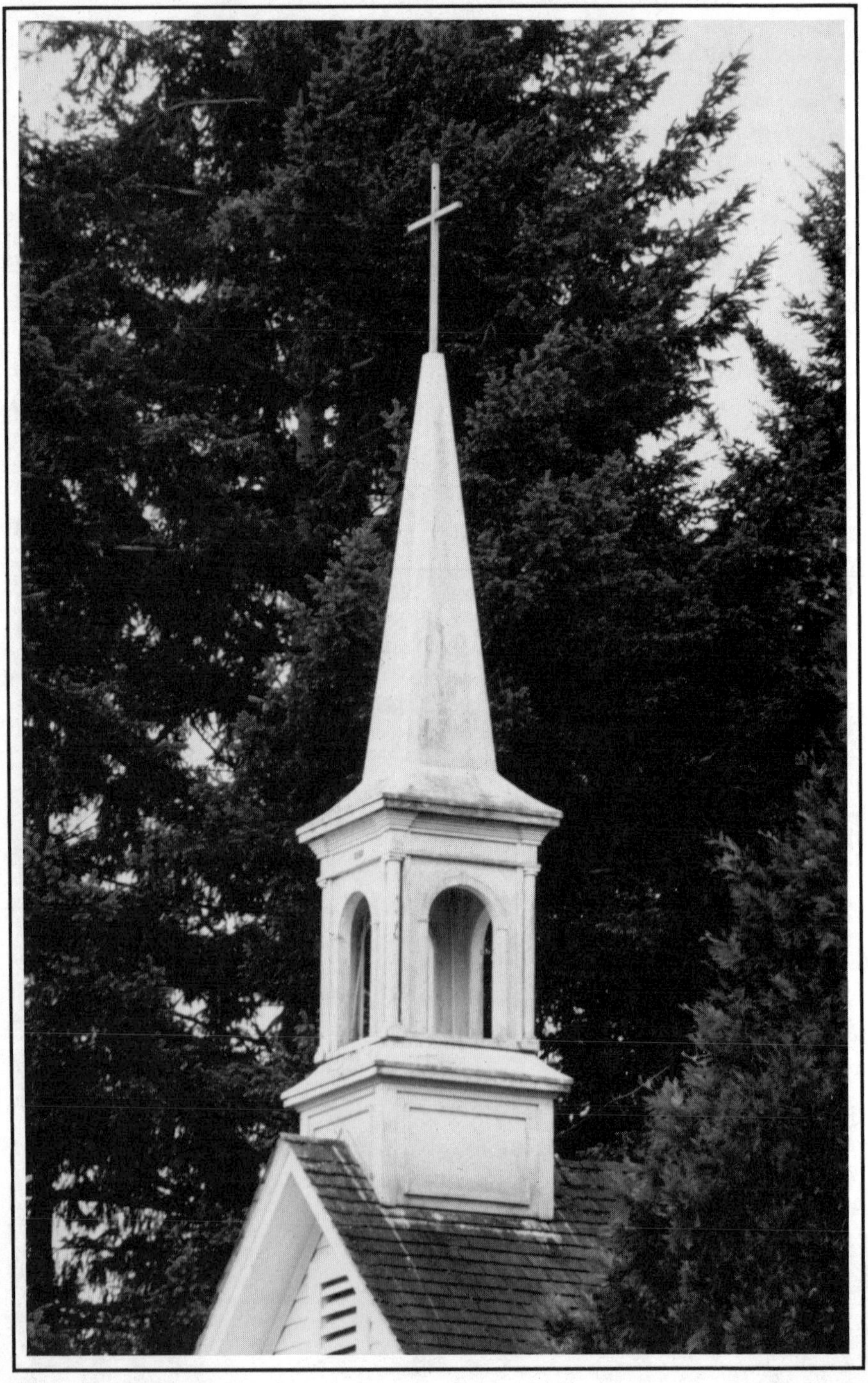

SONGS IN THE NIGHT

Thank God for songs
That speak to our spirits,
Songs that ring a bell
Inside our souls.

Songs that we share,
That bring back memories,
That cause us to smile
And hope and dream.

Songs that lift our faith,
That speak of courage,
That tell us of a bright
Tomorrow.

Songs that share the lyrics
Of love
In words so smooth
We wish
We could have said them.

Thank God for songs
That are special
To us both.
Songs of promise
And loyalty
And faithfulness
And love.

Songs that tell
Of heartbreak
And how people
Rose again
To make life
Work.

Life would be dull
Without the songs
That are special
To both of us.

"Who gives songs in the night."
Job 35:10

THE MONEY SQUEEZE

Don't let the money squeeze
Ruin our love.
Don't let possessions
Tear us apart.

Don't let the lust for things
Guide our lives.
Don't let the thirst for more
Lead us around.

Don't let us argue
From the rising sun
To rising moon
Over dollars, bills,
And credit cards.

It's too easy,
And many of us do.
It's too sad,
And many of us hurt.

Let's share other goals
Of serving,
Of loving,
Of caring,
Of actions
That do not call
For more and more
Money.

Let's find a way
To live each day
Without the continuous
Pressure
Of more money.

Let's find a way
To live beyond
The highs and lows
That only money
Can give.

Let's find a way
To grow a love
That is not a slave
To more money.

"For the love of money is the first
step toward all kinds of sin."   *1 Timothy 6:10, TLB*

$\mathcal{P}$ULLING DOG EARS

What happens when
You grab a dog
By its ears
And hold it off
The ground?

Most dogs will yelp
And howl
And kick their legs
To complain.

Pulling dog ears
Doesn't accomplish much.
It simply makes
The dog miserable
And creates a great deal
Of racket.

What happens when
We break into
Another couple's life?

If they aren't looking
For help
But simply working out
Their own problems,
They feel like dogs
Having their ears pulled.

They are bound
To yelp,
To howl,
And they might even
Try to bite us.

Walk softly into
Someone else's trouble.
We might not be
Needed.
We might not be
Wanted.

And we could
Easily be bitten.

"Like one who seizes a dog by the
ears is a passer-by who meddles in
a quarrel not his own."
            Proverbs 26:17

FIGHT THE LONELINESS

We didn't have to see
The Gulf of Mexico alone.
We didn't have to travel
Plains by ourselves.

We didn't have to sit
In the hospital corridors
With no one to talk to.
We didn't have to watch
The clock tick slowly
All by ourselves.

God gave us each other
To fight back the loneliness.
He gave us a family
To ward off the pain.

Some do not need it.
They stand alone
Like an eagle high
Or an Indian warrior.

But being alone was not
For us,
For being alone drew the
Loneliness.

God gave us each other
So we could hike together,

Be creative partners,
And buck the storm.

God gave us each other
To sleep together,
And shovel walks,
And sit by the
Crackling fire.

Some people may not
Need people;
Other people must have
Loving companionship.

God knew I needed you
To fight the loneliness.

"God sets the lonely in families."
        Psalm 68:6

THE LONG WALK

Thanks for the long walk.
We got to know each other
In a new way.

With aching feet
And screaming arches,
With thighs tied tight
Like walnuts in small bags,
We got to know each other
In a new way.

Twenty-three miles out
And twenty-three miles back
The next day.

We laughed in pain
And spit cotton
From our dry mouths.

We sat—too tired to stand.
We walked—too stiff to sit.

The sight of a dog
Startled us.
Too weary to run,
Too weak to fight,
We dared him to eat us.

We laughed in the rain,
Philosophized in the sunshine,
And collapsed by the roadside,
Too exhausted to think.

We got to know each other
In a new way.

In every experience of life
I get to know you better,
And I appreciate what
An interesting and wise person
God has created.

"He who walks with the wise
grows wise."
Proverbs 13:20

TOO MANY ROLES

Who says men
Can't cook?
Who says women
Can't hammer?

Who says God
Made little
Pigeonholes,
And stuffed
Men in one
And women
In the other?

Some men
Are fantastic
With sewing
Needles.
Some women
Could adjust
An engine
Easily.

A few men
Have been
Known
To guide
A mean
Vacuum cleaner.

More than
One woman
Has hauled
In wood.

Who says God
Made little
Pigeonholes,
And stuffed
Men in one
And women
In the other?

"Once when Jacob was cooking
some stew, Esau came in from the
open country, famished."
                    Genesis 25:29

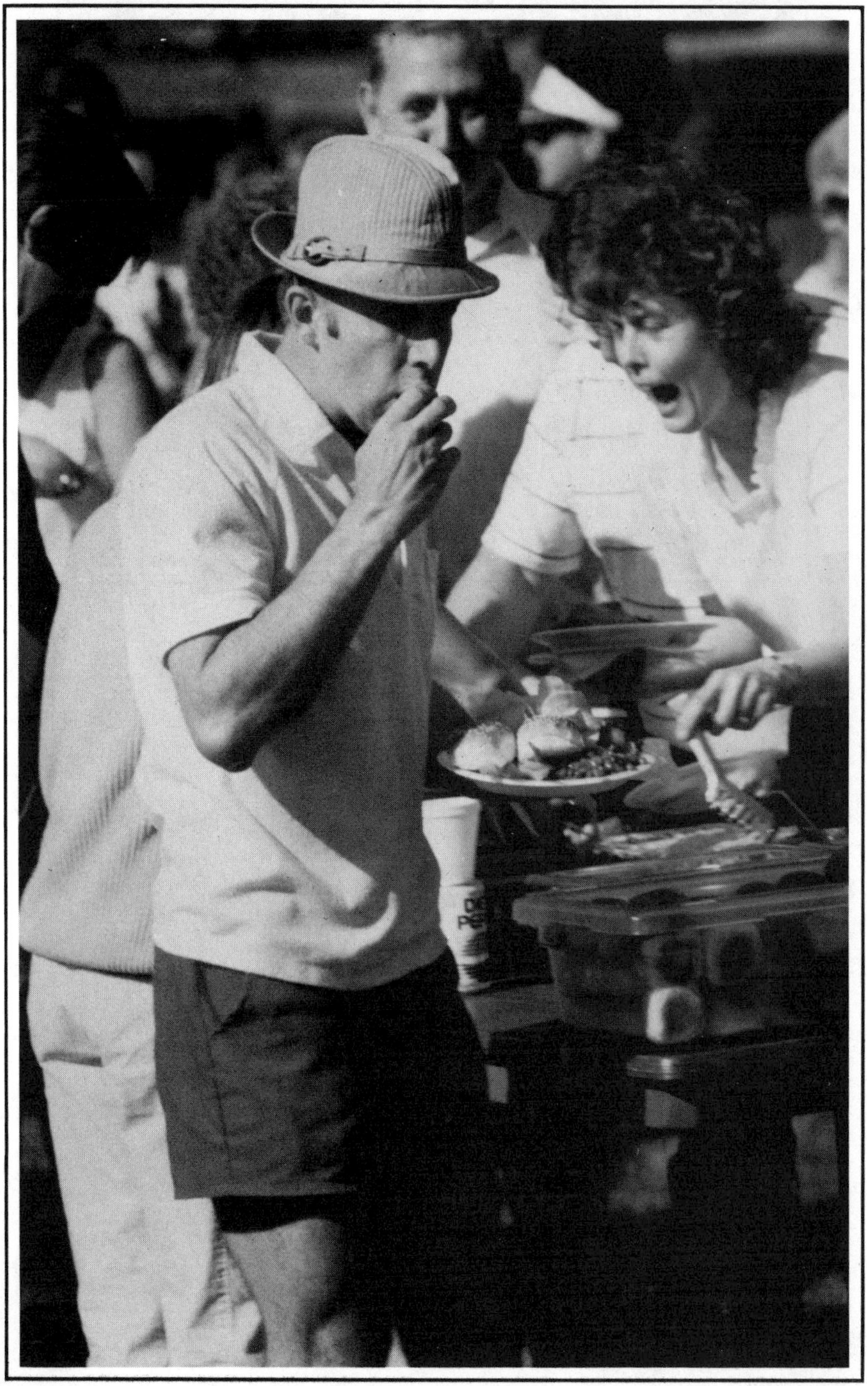

TEARS IN A BOTTLE

Do you ever wonder
What happens to
The tears we shed?

You probably thought
They evaporated
On your cheeks
And the particles
Were washed away.

It would be reasonable
To think that.

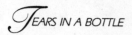

Maybe you thought
We wiped them away
With our sleeves
Or white handkerchiefs
Or the tail of
Our shirts.

It would be reasonable
To think that.

But imagine,
Just imagine,
That God
Lifted every tear
From our face.

Imagine that God
Counted each tear
He collected
And saved them
In a bottle—
One teardrop
At a time.

Imagine that God
Kept track
And cared
About every tear
You and I
Shed.

Picture God
Standing near
To collect
Every tear.

Imagine that
And we will
Come close
To knowing
How much
He cares.

"Thou hast taken account of my
wanderings; put my tears in Thy
bottle; are they not in Thy book?"
                    Psalm 56:8, NASB

ƒOUND OF HIS VOICE

They are hard to live with—
Partners who have learned
To love the sound of
Their own voices.

They know why
The stock market does
What it does
When it does
It.

They know when
The weather will turn—
How it turns
What it turns
To.

They talk and rattle,
Chatter and spat.
They expound and articulate,
Ramble and rave.

These partners who have learned
To love the sound of
Their own voices.

In love with their own opinions,
They seldom stop for air
Or take time to hear
How their partners feel and think.

Smart partners learn to pace,
Take time to breathe,
Swallow and listen.

They respect and hear
Their partner's opinions
Because they realize
Their partner
Is important.

"A fool finds no pleasure in understanding but delights in airing his own opinions."
Proverbs 18:2

$\mathcal{L}$EFT HANGING

*Help me out
When you don't
Feel well.*

*Don't make me guess
What's going on.*

Tell me what's happening.
Are you sick?
Are you tired?
Are you hungry?

Don't leave me hanging.

Tell me what's wrong.
Did I say something?
Did I forget something?
Did I break something?

Don't make me guess
What's going on.

Tell me what made you blue.
Are we broke?
Are we overdue?
Are we drifting?

Don't leave me hanging.

"He was left hanging in midair,
while the mule he was riding kept
on going."

2 Samuel 18:9

BUTTING IN

You were doing fine.
You had everything
Under control
When I decided
To butt in.

I could pretend
I was being helpful,
But instead
I was just being nosy.

I could protest
I was lending
A hand,
But the truth is
I was just intruding.

You had a problem
To resolve
And you would have
Resolved it.

You had a puzzle
To solve
And you would have
Solved it.

I cut you down
By butting in.
I took the ball
Away
By saying you
Couldn't hold it.

I created
A lot of racket,
A gob of turmoil,
A shot of chaos,
A blast of confusion
And
A stretch of tension.

Maybe someday I'll learn
The difference
Between helping
And meddling,
Between encouraging
And butting in.

"Like one who seizes a dog by the
ears is a passer-by who meddles in
a quarrel not his own."
Proverbs 26:17

ATING

After all these years,
After all we've done,
It's still a kick
To go out on a date
With you.

It's still fun to go
For Chinese
And share Mongolian beef

And trade off for
Boiled shrimp.

We still get a charge
Out of sitting close
At a concert
Experiencing something good
Together.

It can't be all work.
It can't be all walls.
It can't be all bills.
It can't be all serve.

Sometimes we need
To stand by the river
And throw in sticks
And watch them
Ride the ripples.

We need to ride horses,
Walk trails,
And listen to robins sing.

We need to get out
And get moving
To keep our date life
Alive
As we keep our love
Alive.

"Enjoy life with your wife."
Ecclesiastes 9:9

*B*EFORE TROUBLE COMES

Trouble is coming
Whether we deserve it
Or not.

No matter how we live,
How optimistic we are,
No matter how we plan,
How cheerful we are.

Trouble comes with
The territory,
For the good
And the bad,
The Christian
And the non.

It's better to tie
Our faith to
Our living God
In the early days.

Better to trust Christ
While life runs
Smoothly.

Trouble is coming
Whether we deserve it
Or not.

While we have
So much
And we smile
So often
And we work
Together,
We need to draw
Our faith in Christ
Together.

And get in the habit
Of trusting
And believing.

Trouble is coming
Whether we deserve it
Or not.

"Remember your Creator in the days
of your youth, before the days of
trouble come and the years
approach when you will say, 'I find
no pleasure in them.'"
                    Ecclesiastes 12:1

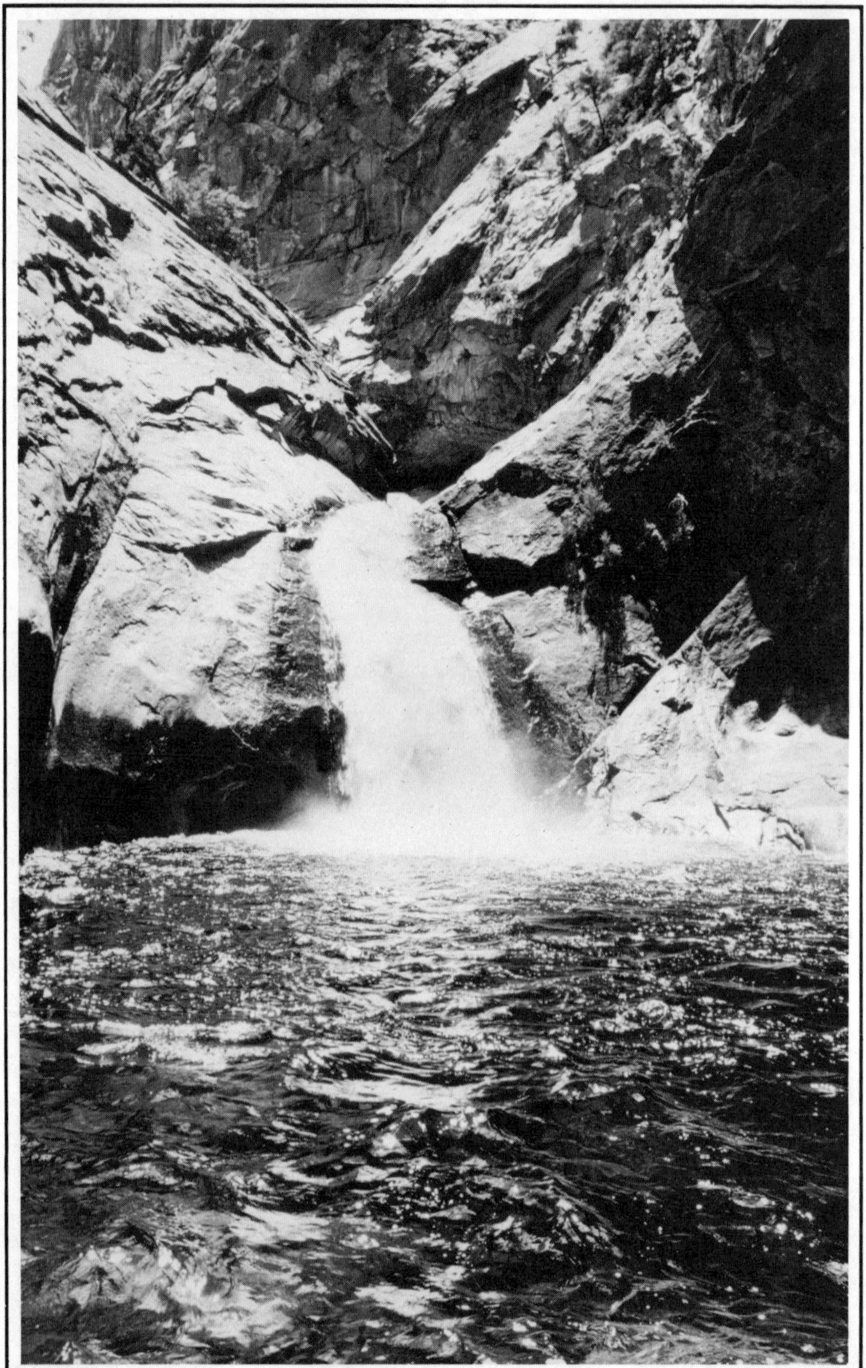

HE HATES TO ADMIT IT

He was a husky worker,
Made his living
With his hands.
The sun had wrinkled
His face.
Cables had toughened
His calloused palms.

For three days he worked
Day and night
To rescue a girl
From a Texas well,
An eighteen-month-old
Lodged twenty-two feet beneath
The earth and rock.

Finally they pulled her
From the jaws of the earth
And she squinted
At the light.

Drillers shouted.
Police cheered.
Newsmen beamed.
Children raced.
Paramedics scurried.

And this worker said,
"I hate to admit it,
But I almost cried."

Go ahead,
Weep with joy.
Let go
And cry aloud.

Don't hold it back.
Let it flow.

Be free and let
Your emotions roll.
Release your feelings
Because God
Has been good.

Let it flow—
For every father,
For every son,
For every husband
Who has bottled
It up too long.

God has been good,
And every man's heart
Can let it flow.

[King David knew how to let go
and weep for happiness:] "Then
they kissed each other and wept
together—but David wept the
most."   *1 Samuel 20:41*

 PACKING LEAVES

You can see her
Half a block away,
Black sack in hand
Scooping leaves
In the autumn sun.

As you drive closer,
She looks up
And waves,
Like a hockey goalie
Half bent over
In the thick
Of the action.

Windblown,
Covered with
Honest dirt,
She smiles
Through her
Dust-caked lips.

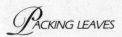

Immediately you know
How it will be.
She will speak
Of joy,
Of happiness,
Of hope,
And her spirit
Will cover you
Like a cool mist.

She went to work,
Started a meal,
And now
She's packing leaves
Like she loves it.

She doesn't leave
Much room for
Doom-and-gloom
Stories.

It's easy to live
With someone who
Thinks packing leaves
Is one of life's
Pleasures.

"Joy and gladness will be found in
her, thanksgiving and the sound of
singing."

Isaiah 51:3

*H*EALING BROKEN HEARTS

Everyone who dares to love
Is bound to feel the pain.

Everyone who dares to care
Will feel the ache inside.

Everyone who feels the joy
Is sure to know the emptiness.

Love has a price to pay.
The price is personal.
The price is high.
The price is deep.
The price is a broken heart.

Everyone who dares to love
Will feel disappointed,
Will feel abused.

He will feel it
From his spouse,
His daughters,
His sons.

Everyone who gives
His heart away
Will have it broken
Sometime.
He can count on it.

But Jesus understands
The risk of loving.
The people He loved
Broke His heart, too.

And Jesus reaches out
To heal
The brokenhearted.

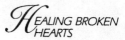
The memories may linger,
But the pain
Can be taken away.

We build again
With the people
We love
Because Jesus
Heals the brokenhearted.

"He has sent me to bind up the
brokenhearted."
                    Isaiah 61:1

ACIAL OIL

Cosmetics are big business,
Always have been,
Probably always will be.

They darken the eyes,
Contour the cheeks,
Highlight the lips,
Maybe hide a crow's-foot
Or two.

Sometimes they accent
An outfit,
Possibly take a shadow
Off a chin.

But every face
Needs a good base
That no one
Can buy.

Beautiful women
Always begin
With a joy within
Called the oil of gladness.

Beautiful women
Are happy
In their hearts
And it shows
On their faces.

*" . . . to bestow on them a crown of
beauty . . . the oil of gladness . . .
and a garment of praise . . ."*
Isaiah 61:3

WHAT DO MEN WANT?

What do men want
Most in life?
These strange beings
Caught up in egos,
Power plays
And status symbols.

Deep in their hearts
Where they let few visit
And almost no one stay,
What do they long for?
What do they crave
To make life complete?

At the core most men
Cry out for
An undying love.
For someone who
Cares no matter what.
For someone who
Is dependable whatever
The circumstances.

Not someone who
Will tolerate abuse,
But someone
Who will be patient
When they are strong
And when they are

Weak.
Someone who will
Stand with them
In the sunshine
And
In the darkness.

Isn't that what
All of us want—
Someone to care
In the sunshine
And
In the darkness?

"What a man desires is unfailing love."
Proverbs 19:22

PRISONERS OF HOPE!

Sometimes we want
To give up,
Throw in the towel
And call it
A nice try.

It doesn't last
Long,
But every now
And again
It's there.

But God
Has not let us
Stray very far
From hope.

He sends us
Reminders
Of what
Our love means
To us.

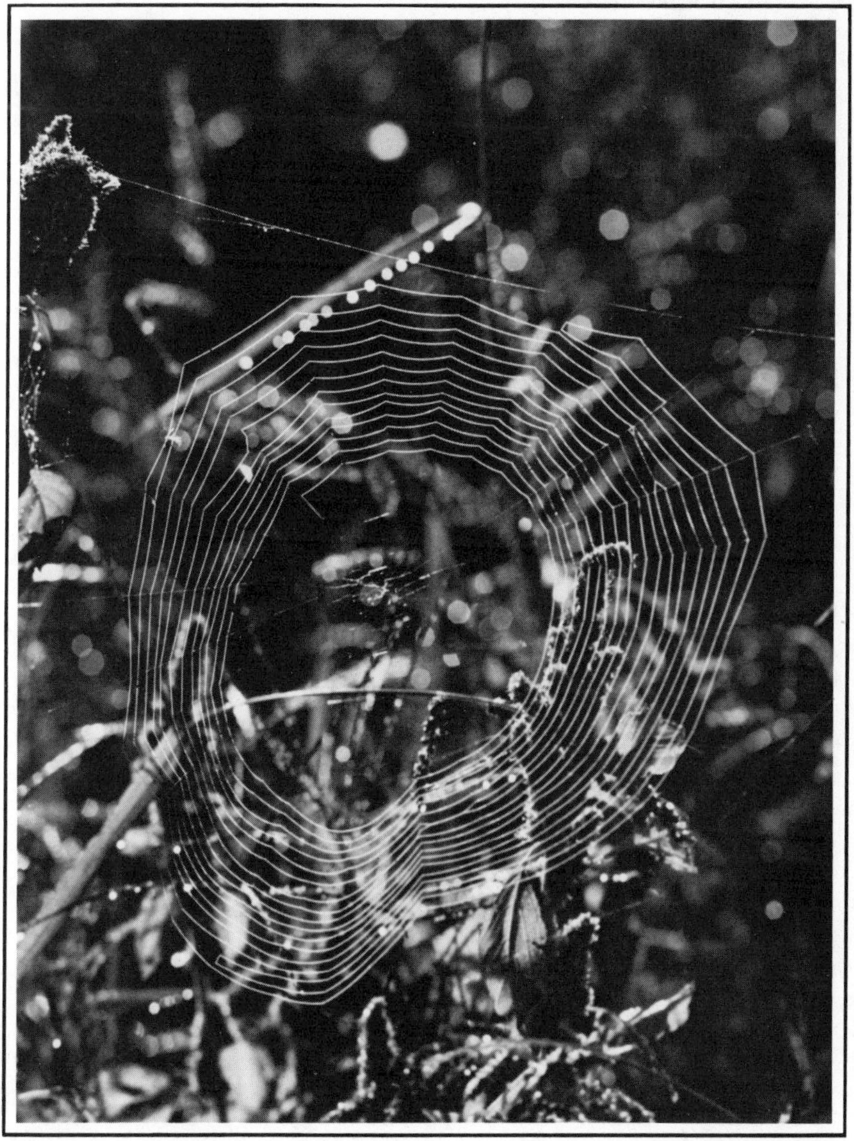

We have not
Been able to
Get away
From each
Other
Because love
Keeps calling
Us back,
And we
Are thankful.

We are prisoners,
Prisoners of Hope.
And hope
Will not
Let us go.

It is one
Of the few
Prisons
I can
Be grateful for,
Because you make
A fantastic
Cell mate.

"Return to your fortress, O prisoners
of hope."

Zechariah 9:12